What is Kumon?

Kumon is the world's largest supplemental education provider and a leader in producing outstanding results. After-school programs in math and reading at Kumon Centers around the globe have been helping children succeed for 50 years.

Kumon Workbooks represent just a fraction of our complete curriculum of preschool-to-college-level material assigned at Kumon Centers under the supervision of trained Kumon Instructors.

The Kumon Method enables each child to progress successfully by practicing material until concepts are mastered and advancing in small, manageable increments. Instructors carefully assign materials and pace advancement according to the strengths and needs of each individual student.

Students usually attend a Kumon Center twice a week and practice at home the other five days. Assignments take about twenty minutes.

Kumon helps students of all ages and abilities master the basics, improve concentration and study habits, and build confidence.

How did Kumon begin?

IT ALL BEGAN IN JAPAN 50 YEARS AGO when a parent and teacher named Toru Kumon found a way to help his son Takeshi do better in school. At the prompting of his wife, he created a series of short assignments that his son could complete successfully in less than 20 minutes a day and that would ultimately make high school math easy. Because each was just a bit more challenging than the last, Takeshi was able to master the skills and gain the confidence to keep advancing.

This unique self-learning method was so successful that Toru's son was able to do calculus by the time he was in the sixth grade. Understanding the value of good reading comprehension, Mr. Kumon then developed a reading program employing the same method. His programs are the basis and inspiration of those offered at Kumon Centers today under the expert guidance of professional Kumon Instructors.

Mr. Toru Kumon
Founder of Kumon

What can Kumon do for my child?

Kumon is geared to children of all ages and skill levels. Whether you want to give your child a leg up in his or her schooling, build a strong foundation for future studies or address a possible learning problem, Kumon provides an effective program for developing key learning skills given the strengths and needs of each individual child.

What makes Kumon so different?

Kumon uses neither a classroom model nor a tutoring approach. It's designed to facilitate self-acquisition of the skills and study habits needed to improve academic performance. This empowers children to succeed on their own, giving them a sense of accomplishment that fosters further achievement. Whether for remedial work or enrichment, a child advances according to individual ability and initiative to reach his or her full potential. Kumon is not only effective, but also surprisingly affordable.

What is the role of the Kumon Instructor?

Kumon Instructors regard themselves more as mentors or coaches than teachers in the traditional sense. Their principal role is to provide the direction, support and encouragement that will guide the student to performing at 100% of his or her potential. Along with their rigorous training in the Kumon Method, all Kumon Instructors share a passion for education and an earnest desire to help children succeed.

KUMON FOSTERS:

- A mastery of the basics of reading and math
- Improved concentration and study habits
- Increased self-discipline and self-confidence
- A proficiency in material at every level
- Performance to each student's full potential
- A sense of accomplishment

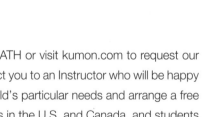

▶▶ GETTING STARTED IS EASY. Just call us at 800.ABC.MATH or visit kumon.com to request our free brochure and find a Kumon Center near you. We'll direct you to an Instructor who will be happy to speak with you about how Kumon can address your child's particular needs and arrange a free placement test. There are more than 1,400 Kumon Centers in the U.S. and Canada, and students may enroll at any time throughout the year, even summer. Contact us today.

FIND OUT MORE ABOUT KUMON MATH & READING CENTERS.
Receive a free copy of our parent guide, *Every Child an Achiever,* by visiting
kumon.com/go.survey or calling 800.ABC.MATH.

 **Apple**

Cut out the part at the bottom and paste it onto the illustration above to complete the picture.

 **3** **Orange**

■ Cut out the part at the bottom and paste it onto the illustration above to complete the picture.

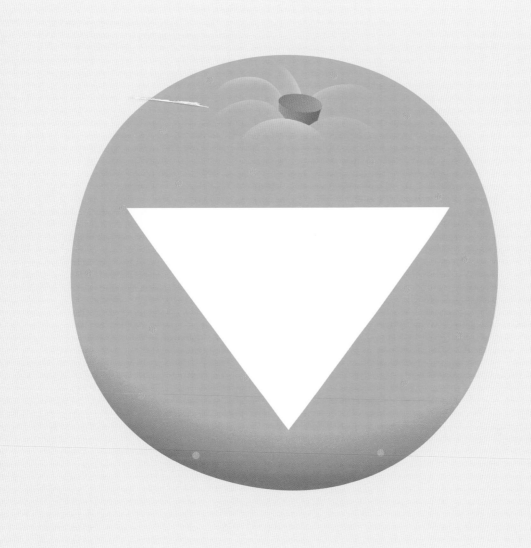

4 Cucumber

■ Cut out the part on the right and paste it onto the illustration on the left to complete the picture.

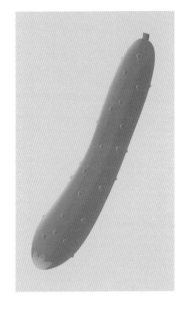

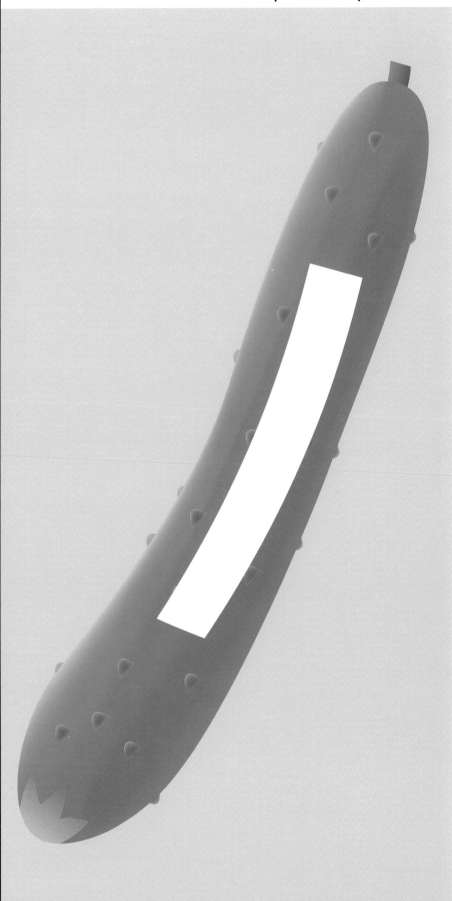

To parents
The shape of this part may be difficult for children to cut out precisely. It is not a problem if what your child has cut is a little askew. Offer lots of praise for his or her effort in learning to cut and paste. If your child seems to have difficulty cutting out the part, you can offer to help and then encourage him or her to paste it onto the illustration.

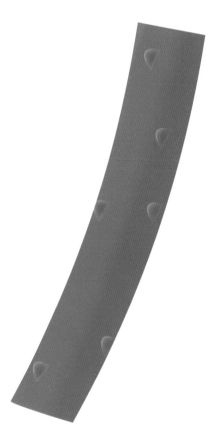

 **Pig**

To parents
Starting with this page, your child will learn to arrange the facial features of animals. You can encourage him or her to try and put the parts onto suitable places to see what the face will look like before pasting them. Offer lots of praise for his or her effort.

■ Cut out the parts at the bottom and paste them onto the pig's face.

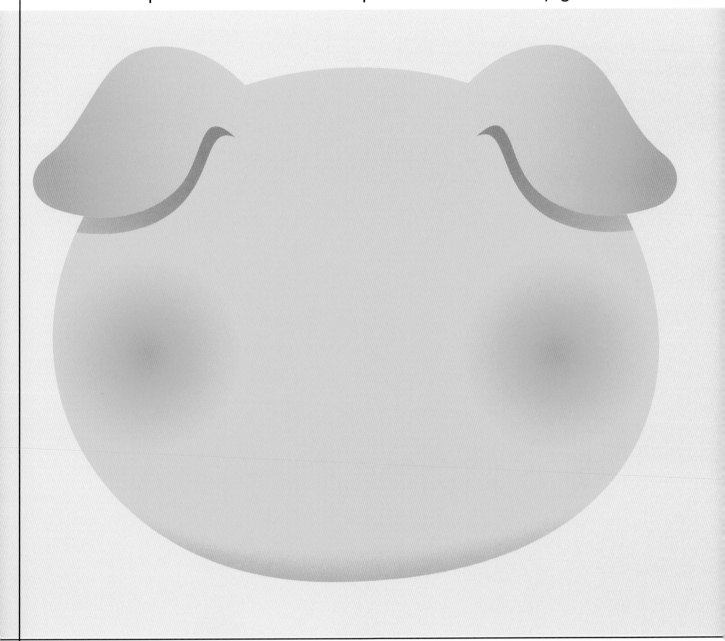

 # Gorilla

■ Cut out the parts at the bottom and paste them onto the gorilla's face.

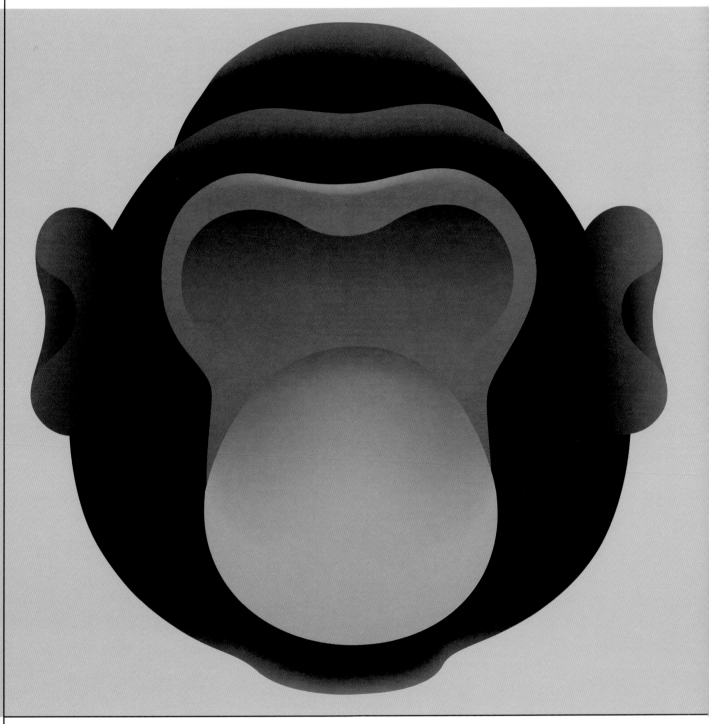

7 Teatime

To parents
Please encourage your child to look carefully at the sample illustration on the right. Offer lots of praise when the picture is completed.

■ Cut out the parts at the bottom and paste them onto the illustration as shown above.

8 Let's Eat!

■ Cut out the parts at the bottom and paste them onto the illustration as shown above.

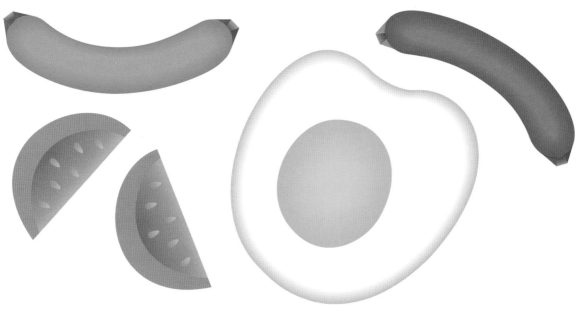

9 Let's Skate!

■ Cut out the parts at the bottom and paste them onto the illustration as shown above.

 **Let's Play Baseball!**

■ Cut out the parts at the bottom and paste them onto the illustration as shown above.

11 You Look a Little Strange...

To parents
Please encourage your child to look carefully at the sample illustration on the right. There are glue marks on projects 11-15. Have your child place glue on the marks. Offer lots of praise when the picture is completed.

■ Cut out the parts on the right and paste them onto matching animals.

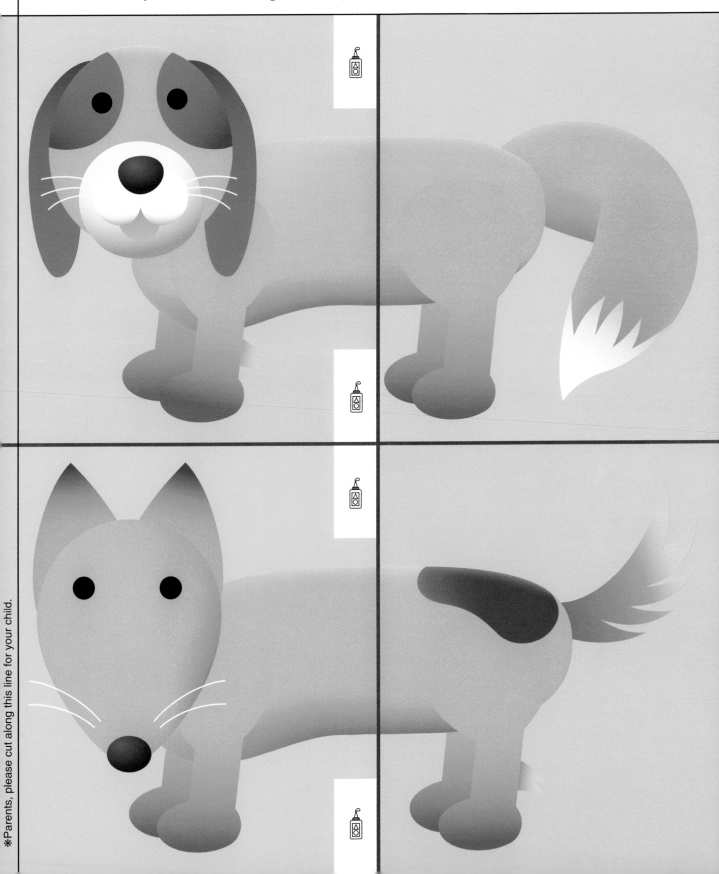

*Parents, please cut along this line for your child.

You Look a Little Strange...

■ Cut out the parts on the right and paste them onto matching animals.

 **13** **You Look a Little Strange...**

■Cut out the parts on the right and paste them onto matching animals.

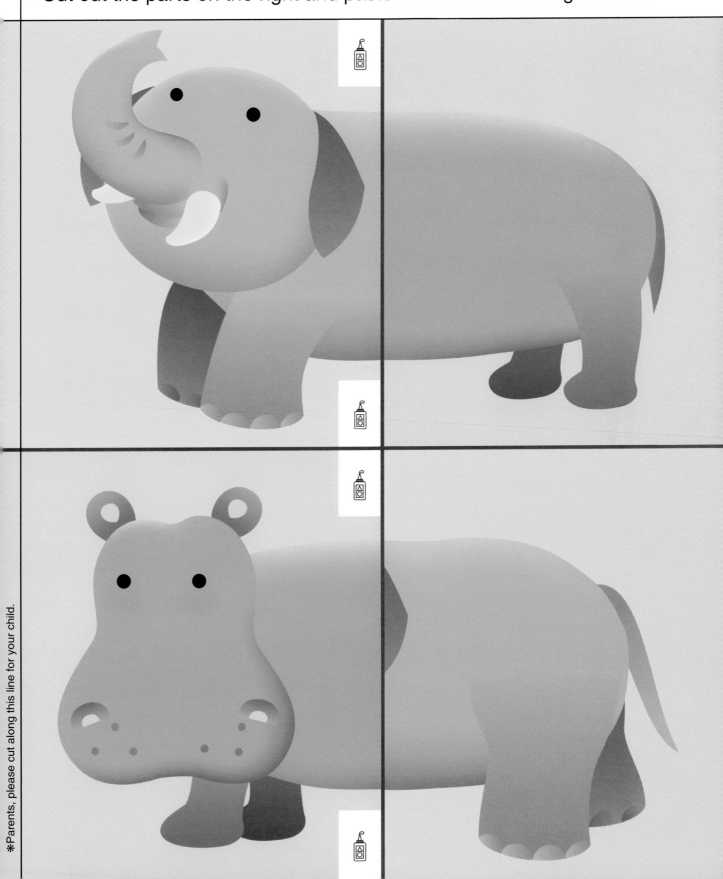

You Look a Little Strange...

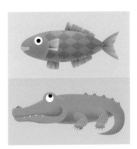

■ Cut out the parts on the right and paste them onto matching animals.

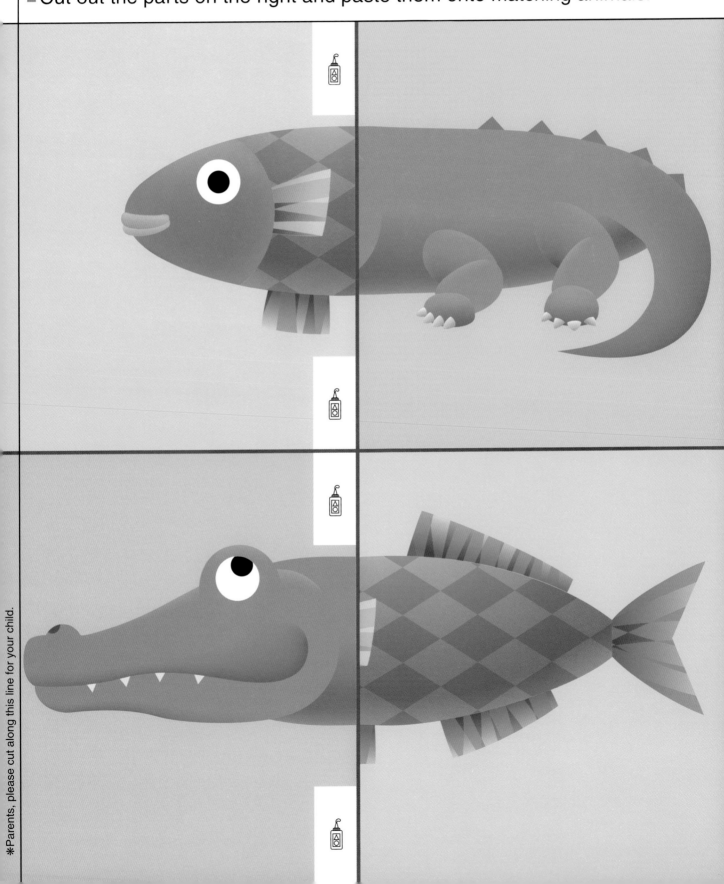

■ Cut out the parts at the bottom and paste them onto matching animals.

*Parents, please cut along this line for your child.

16 **Bulldog**

To parents
In projects 16-21, your child will practice pasting one piece onto another piece. Have your child paste each piece onto its corresponding number in numerical order. If your child has difficulty deciding where to paste the pieces, you can offer to paste a couple pieces to give your child a hint.

■ Cut out the parts at the bottom and paste them in numerical order onto the illustration as shown above.

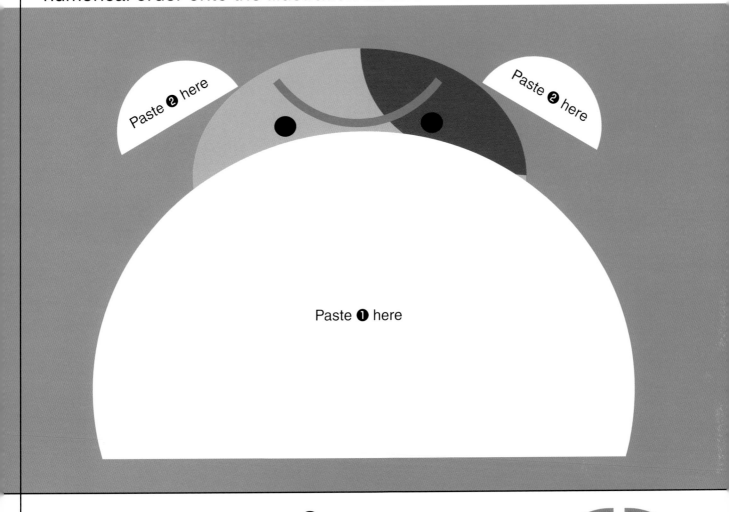

Paste ❷ here

Paste ❷ here

Paste ❶ here

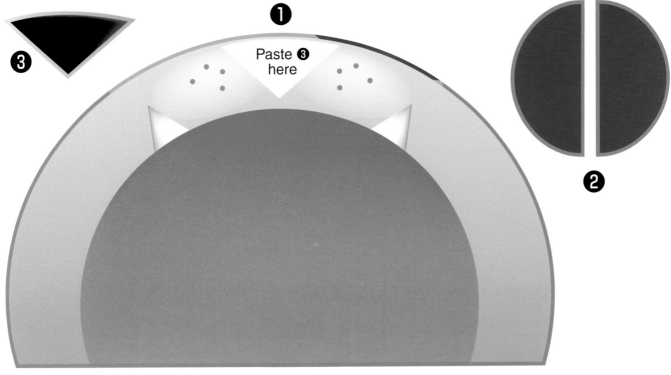

❸

❶

Paste ❸ here

❷

*Parents, please cut along this line for your child.

 # Tiger

■Cut out the parts at the bottom and paste them in numerical order onto the illustration as shown above.

Paste ❷ here

Paste ❷ here

Paste ❶ here

 ❶

❷

❸

 Paste ❸ here

Paste ❹ here

❹

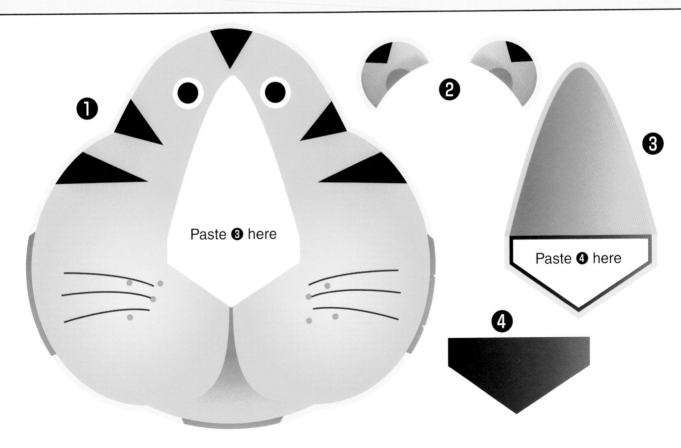

✳Parents, please cut along this line for your child.

Cut out the parts at the bottom and paste them in numerical order onto the illustration as shown above.

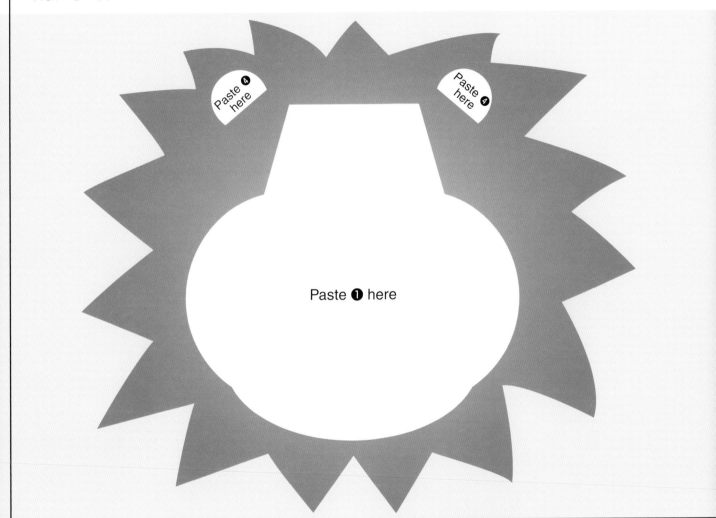

Paste ❶ here

Paste ❹ here

Paste ❹ here

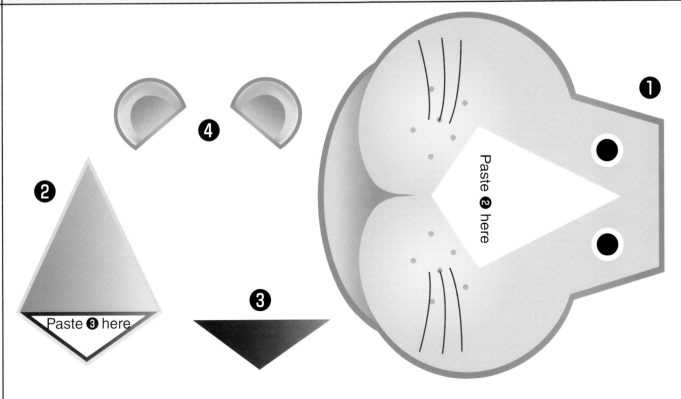

❶

Paste ❷ here

❷

Paste ❸ here

❸

❹

 **Raccoon**

■ Cut out the parts at the bottom and paste them in numerical order onto the illustration as shown above.

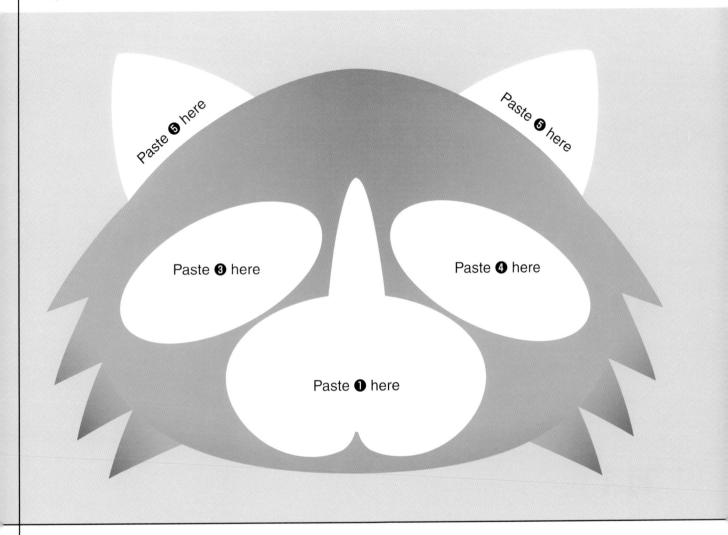

Paste ❺ here

Paste ❺ here

Paste ❸ here

Paste ❹ here

Paste ❶ here

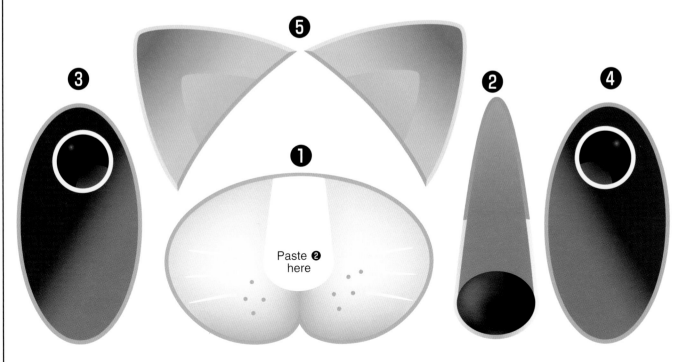

❺

❸

❶

Paste ❷ here

❷

❹

■Cut out the parts at the bottom and paste them in numerical order onto the illustration as shown above.

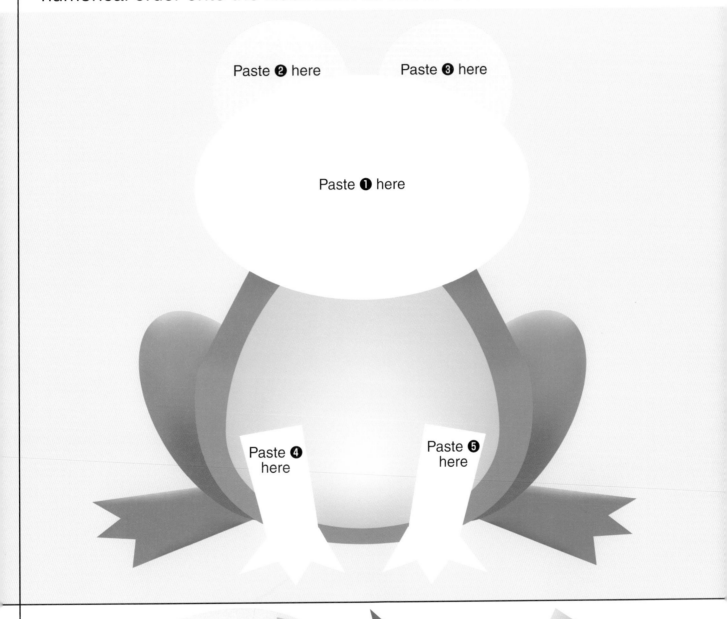

Paste ❷ here Paste ❸ here

Paste ❶ here

Paste ❹ here Paste ❺ here

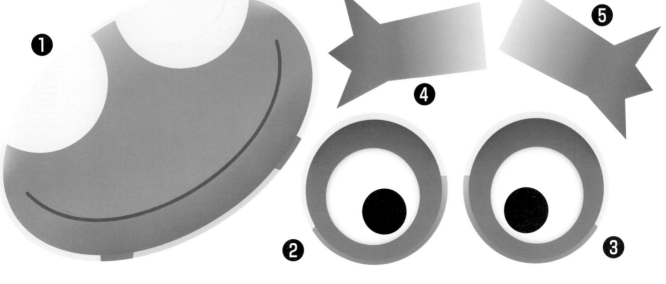

❶ ❺ ❹ ❷ ❸

 **Eagle**

■ Cut out the parts at the bottom and paste them in numerical order onto the illustration as shown above.

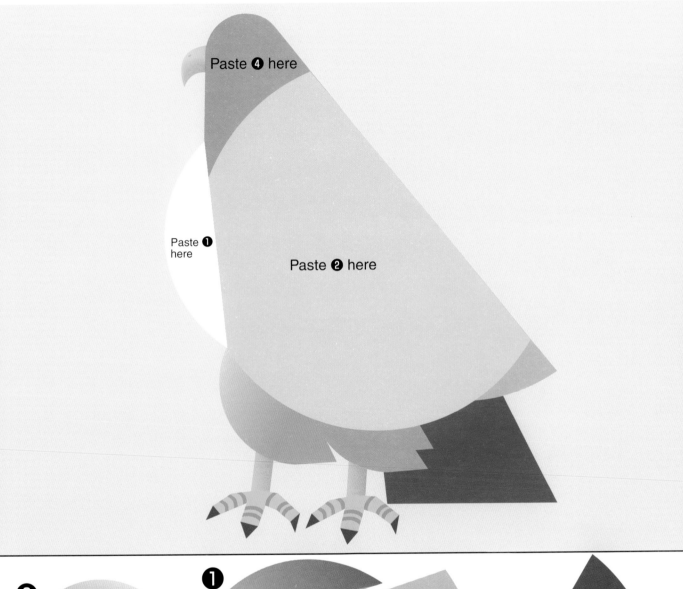

Paste ❹ here

Paste ❶ here

Paste ❷ here

❸

❶

Paste ❺ here

Paste ❸ here

❷

❹

❺

Doctor

■ Cut out the parts at the bottom and paste them onto the illustration above to complete the picture.

Police Officer

Cut out the parts at the bottom and paste them onto the illustration above to complete the picture.

Firefighter

Cut out the parts at the bottom and paste them onto the illustration above to complete the picture.

25 Basketball Player

■ Cut out the parts at the bottom and paste them onto the illustration above to complete the picture.

Football Player

■ Cut out the parts at the bottom and paste them onto the illustration above to complete the picture.

Baseball Player

■ Cut out the parts at the bottom and paste them onto the illustration above to complete the picture.

What's on the Tree?

■ Cut out the parts at the bottom and paste them onto the illustration above to complete the picture.

In the Sea

■ Cut out the parts at the bottom
and paste them onto the illustration
above to complete the picture.

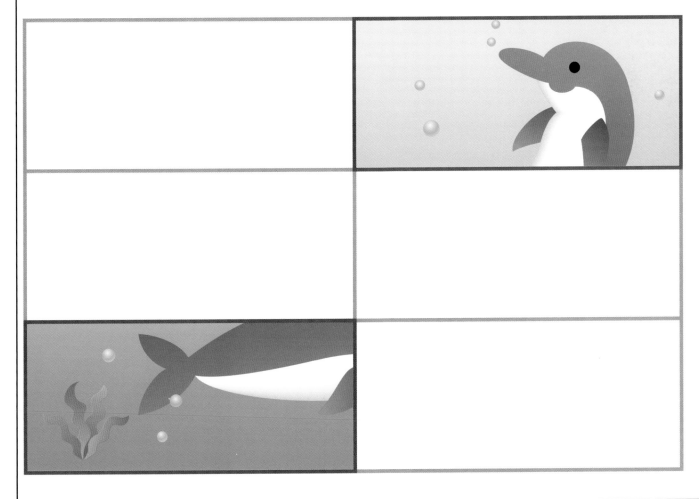

30 At the Fair

■ Cut out the parts at the bottom and paste them onto the illustration above to complete the picture.

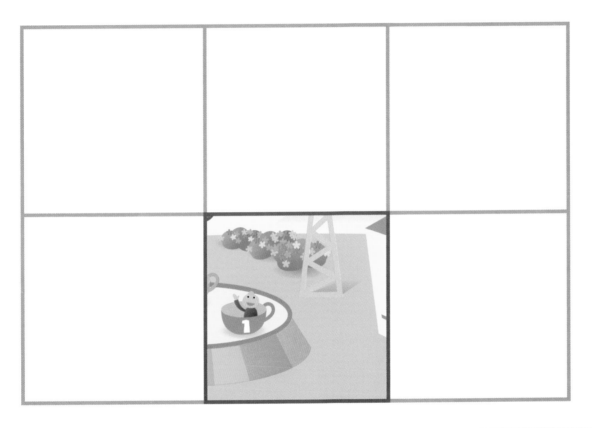

31 At the Circus

■ Cut out the parts at the bottom
and paste them onto the illustration
above to complete the picture.

32 Marching Band

■ Cut out the parts at the bottom and paste them onto the illustration above to complete the picture.

33 Flower

■ Cut out the parts at the bottom and paste them onto the illustration above to complete the picture.

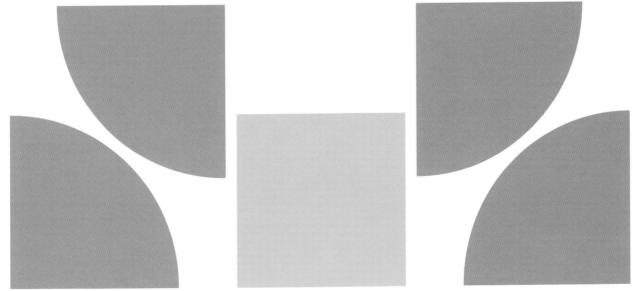

34 Star

To parents
From this page on, your child will learn to arrange and combine different shapes to complete pictures. Have your child combine the parts to complete the picture as shown on the right. If your child has difficulty, give him or her hints.

■ Cut out the parts at the bottom and paste them onto the illustration above to complete the picture.

35 Heart

■ Cut out the parts at the bottom and paste them onto the illustration above to complete the picture.

Space Shuttle

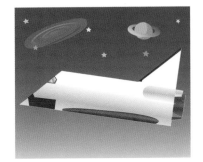

■ Cut out the parts at the bottom and paste them onto the illustration above to complete the picture.

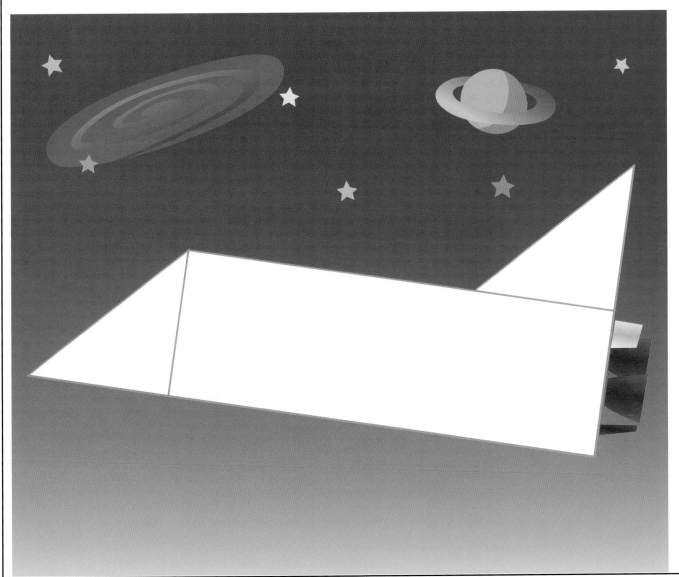

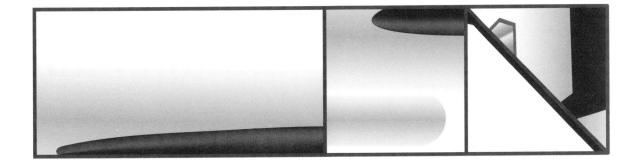

37 Cat

■ Cut out the parts at the bottom and paste them onto the illustration above to complete the picture.

Angelfish

■ Cut out the parts at the bottom and paste them onto the illustration above to complete the picture.

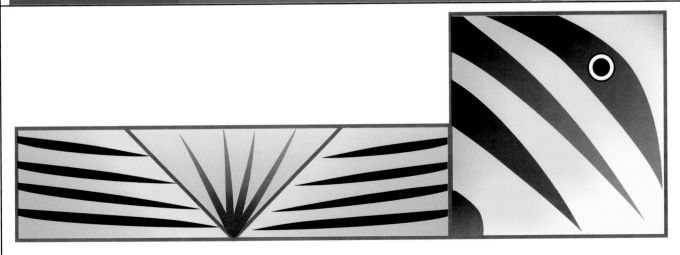

39 Kangaroo

■ Cut out the parts at the bottom and paste them onto the illustration above to complete the picture.

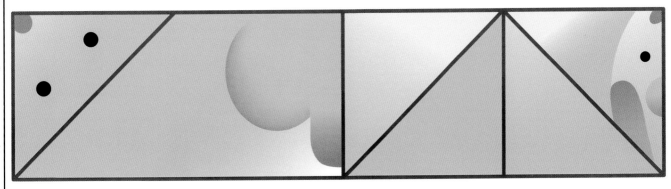

 **House**

To parents
Has your child enjoyed cutting and pasting? Please give lots of praise for his or her effort and achievement.

■ Cut out the parts at the bottom and paste them onto the illustration above to complete the picture.

*Parents, please cut along this line for your child.

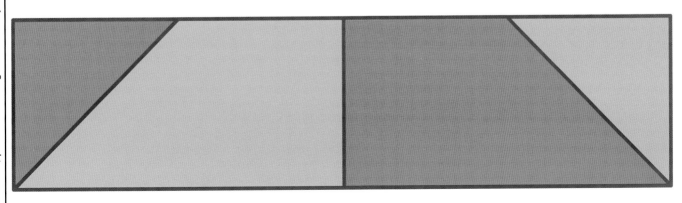

KUM◯N

Certificate of Achievement

is hereby congratulated on completing

My Book of Pasting

Presented on _____ , 20 ___

_____
Parent or Guardian